THE DINOSAUR
WHO DISCOVERED
HAMBURGERS
2

CUTTING THE BIG CHEESE

Scout the dinosaur was very happy with the discovery of hamburgers.

Scout the dinosaur
HAMBURGER DISCOVERER

Ever since that day, Scout had become the most famous dinosaur to have ever lived.

Scout appeared on talk shows,

in newspapers,

and was celebrated by dinosaurs everywhere.

One day, Scout was sailing to the opening of a new hamburger restaurant on an island nearby when a terrible storm took the boat off course.

Scout fought hard to try and keep the boat afloat while the waves threw it side to side.

The heavy rain, crashing waves and night sky made it difficult to see...

...until suddenly Scout's boat was washed ashore.

Scout awoke on a deserted island in an ancient part of the world that had not been explored for thousands of years.

The island was full of wonder!
Scout grabbed the trusty
adventure gear and set off.

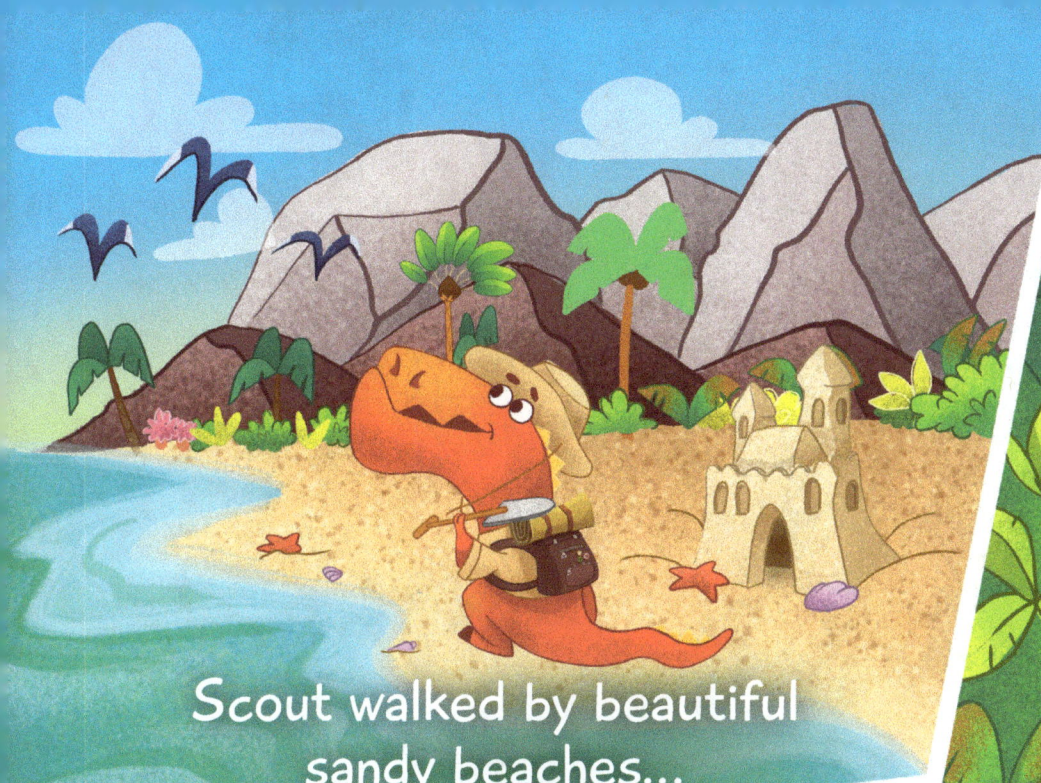

Scout walked by beautiful sandy beaches...

pushed through spiky hedges...

and paddled through rushing river rapids.

Scout finally reached what looked like a jungle full of trees. But there was a strange smell in the air.

Scout picked what looked like some kind of odd fruit, but was surprised that it was actually smelly and gooey.

OF COURSE!

These were Aged Cheese Trees!

Excitedly, Scout tasted it and thought to take a sample of the smelly cheese and continued the adventure.

Scout then began to climb a mountain and found all the adventure gear was getting covered with something blue.

Upon inspection, Scout realized it was cheese that was covering everything!
OF COURSE!
This was a Blue Cheese Mountain!

Intrigued by this, Scout collected some
of the blue cheese and ventured on.

Next, Scout found a meadow covered
by a gorgeous white shimmer.

OF COURSE!

These were White Cheese Lilies!

Scout grabbed a bushel and kept going.

Finally, Scout stumbled upon a hidden cave with a mysterious glow coming from within.

Scout entered and saw a golden
wheel at the end of the room shining
brightly like a piece of gold.

Scout started to walk closer and noticed there were strange markings on the floor.

Scout stepped on one...

SWOOSHHH

an arrow shot out from the wall and narrowly missed!

The room was set with traps.
Scout had to avoid the traps
and get to the end of the room.

Scout got to the end and came
up to the large golden wheel.
Scout couldn't believe it...
the legend was true!

OF COURSE!

This was the Great Wheel
of Cheddar Cheese!

Legends of CHEESE

It was written about in history books
but dinosaurs thought it was just a myth!

Scout cut a piece of the cheese to taste it.
MMMMMM.

Now that was REALLY something, unlike anything
Scout had ever tasted before. That melty, gooey,
cheesy goodness of the cheddar cheese had to be
shared with the world!

Scout cut a big round piece of the
Great Wheel of Cheddar Cheese
and headed back.

Scout had a long way back home...

through the cave...

through the white cheese meadow...

down the blue cheese mountain...

past the aged cheese trees...

...paddling through the rushing river rapids...

pushing past the spiky hedges...

and walking again along the sandy beaches to the boat.

Scout got the boat back in the water...

...and navigated the ship back home.

Scout got back into the kitchen and set up a cheese board with all the different cheeses that had been discovered.

Scout invited Dr. Chee Burger, Dr. Ham's cousin, who was an expert scientist in all things cheesy and delicious.

They tried all the different types of cheese and took notes about how they taste and what they can be paired with.

Some cheeses were better with crackers.

Some were better with fruit.

And some were just better on their own.

But Dr. Chee asked Scout to make one of those famous hamburgers everyone loved, to test something out.

As Scout began to put the ingredients together, Dr. Chee put a new ingredient into the mix:

Bun

Ketchup

Pickles

Bacon

Cheddar Cheese!?!

Patty

Mustard

and Bun

Dr. Chee had cut the cheese without Scout realizing!
They both tried the new hamburger and looked at
each other in disbelief. It was so delicious that they
didn't know what to say except

"The world needs to try this!"

The next day Scout went on another talk show and introduced the new hamburger to the world.

It became all the rage and dinosaurs from all around the world had to try this new variation.

Upon taking a bite, the critics were amazed by the taste and immediately gave it another 6 Claws way up!

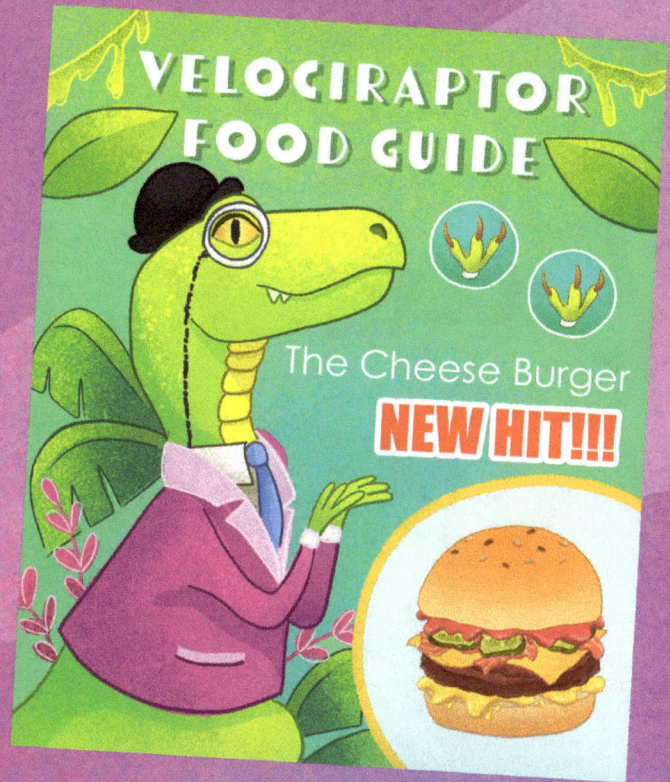

VELOCIRAPTOR FOOD GUIDE

The Cheese Burger

NEW HIT!!!

When Scout was asked what this new burger would be called, Scout said, "The Cheese Burger!" Afterall, Dr. Chee Burger put cheese in a burger! Everyone was amazed by Scout's genius.

CHEESE BURGER

With the approval of Dr. Chee and the Velociraptor Food Guide, Scout's discovery became the talk of the town.

From that day on, hamburgers with cheddar cheese were enjoyed by all the dinosaurs in the world, and Scout was celebrated as a true culinary adventurer.

Scout felt happy and complete.
The perfect dish was even better
and all was right in the world.

Read all of "The Animal Who" series!

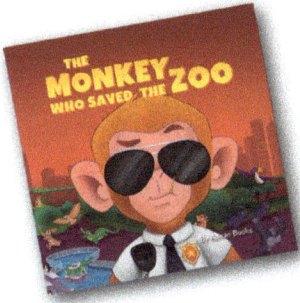

THE MONKEY WHO SAVED THE ZOO

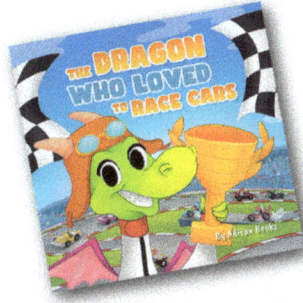

THE DRAGON WHO LOVED TO RACE CARS

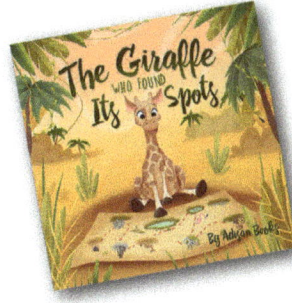

The Giraffe Who Found Its Spots

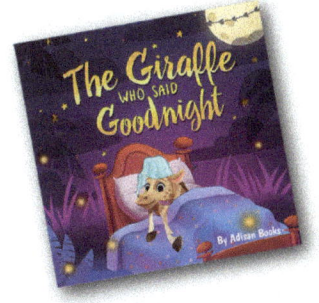

The Giraffe Who Said Goodnight

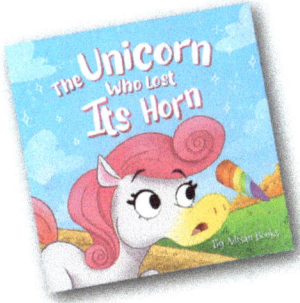

The Unicorn Who Lost Its Horn

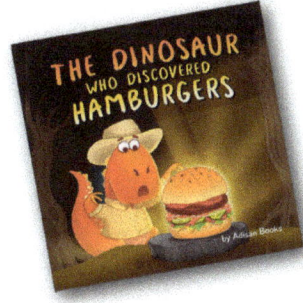

THE DINOSAUR WHO DISCOVERED HAMBURGERS

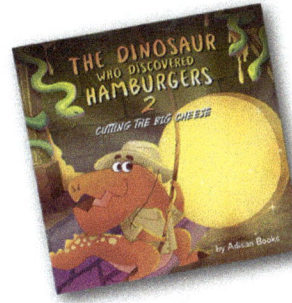

THE DINOSAUR WHO DISCOVERED HAMBURGERS 2

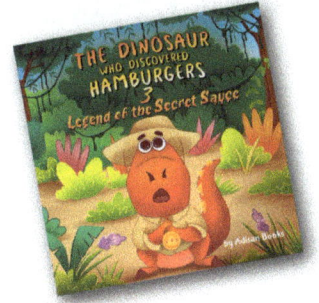

THE DINOSAUR WHO DISCOVERED HAMBURGERS 3 Legend of the Secret Sauce

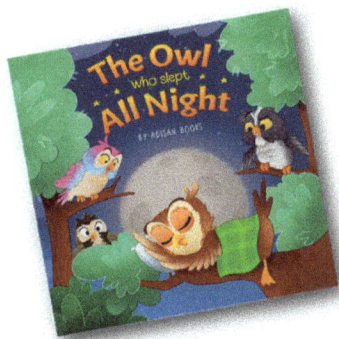

The Owl Who Slept All Night

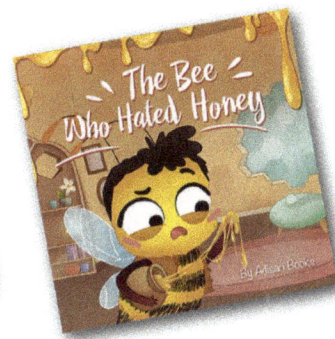

The Bee Who Hated Honey

Available on Amazon

www.ingramcontent.com/pod-product-compliance
Lightning Source LLC
Chambersburg PA
CBHW062007090426
42811CB00005B/777